My Own Reflections II

by
Peter Vallas

Trafford
PUBLISHING™

Order this book online at www.trafford.com/08-0885
or email orders@trafford.com

Most Trafford titles are also available at major online book retailers.

Edited by: Karen Larvin
Cover Photography by: Emily Jerome

Note for Librarians: A cataloguing record for this book is available from Library
and Archives Canada at www.collectionscanada.ca/amicus/index-e.html

Printed in Victoria, BC, Canada.

ISBN: 978-1-4251-8266-3

Trafford rev. 6/15/2009

*We at Trafford believe that it is the responsibility of us all, as both individuals
and corporations, to make choices that are environmentally and socially sound.
You, in turn, are supporting this responsible conduct each time you purchase a
Trafford book, or make use of our publishing services. To find out how you are
helping, please visit www.trafford.com/responsiblepublishing.html*

*Our mission is to efficiently provide the world's finest, most comprehensive
book publishing service, enabling every author to experience success.
To find out how to publish your book, your way, and have it available
worldwide, visit us online at www.trafford.com/10510*

www.trafford.com

North America & international
toll-free: 1 888 232 4444 (USA & Canada)
phone: 250 383 6864 ◆ fax: 250 383 6804
email: info@trafford.com

The United Kingdom & Europe
phone: +44 (0)1865 487 395 ◆ local rate: 0845 230 9601
facsimile: +44 (0)1865 481 507 ◆ email: info.uk@trafford.com

10 9 8 7 6 5 4 3 2

The Author

My Own Reflections II, is Peter Vallas's expressions of life. His poems are warm and human, revealing a gentle and congenial person. Some are serious; others whimsical, in all of them his words display the depth of his feelings. He is one of the most inspiring poets of the day.

His poems have been published in magazines and on cards. As an author, in "Lyrical Voices" and anthology published in 1979 by Young Publishing Company, his work was well received.

All references to "Rhoda" are to his wife, who uses her Greek name of "Eleni" in her daily life.

He was published in 1981 in "The World's Great Contemporary Poems."
He was published in "Our World's Best Loved Poems," and in 1995 he was published in "A Delicate Balance," by The National Library of Poetry. He was a member of International Society of Poets in 1995-1996.

Awards – World of Poetry

Golden Poet Award	1985-1987-1988-1989
Silver Poet Award	1986
Award of Merit	1983
Four Awards of Merit	1987

Editor's Choice Award – National Library of Poetry   1995

Letters of Acknowledgement

President Gerald Ford	1979-1981
President Jimmy Carter	1981
The Prince and Princess of Wales	1981

Elizabeth Taylor	1984
Bill Marriott, Jr.	1988
Henry A. Kissinger	1982
Pope John Paul	1981
Governor Mario M. Cuomo	1986
Governor Hugh Carey	1981
Former Hostage Kathryn Koob	1981
Dr. Norman Vincent Peale	1982
Honorable Strom Thurmond	1982

Not only does he reflect life as he sees it with words, Peter Vallas, is an accomplished artist, working in oils. He paints life as he writes poems, with deep understanding and clarity.

Peter Vallas has been in the fire service since 1961, rising from firefighter to Captain and then Fire Marshal. President Jimmy Carter commended Peter in 1977, for having saved thirty-seven lives during his career. His present record is over forty-two lives saved to date and is one of the most decorated firefighters in The United States.

In 1982, Peter received "The American Character Award" in Washington, D.C., at a ceremony in The Russell Senate Office Building at the Caucus Room. He was given a reception of honor. It was attended by many elected officials, as well as Representatives of the Military and Diplomatic Corps. In attendance were Honorable Strom Thurmond, President Pro Tem of the U.S. Senate and Chairman of the Senate Judiciary Committee, Mr. Rand Araskog, Chairman and President of IT&T, and Doctor Norman Vincent Peale.

Peter is also an accomplished actor and a member of The Screen Actors Guild.

CONTENTS

DEDICATION

This book of inspirations is dedicated to my loving wife, Eleni, whose support and love continues to inspire my feelings to write. She has always been my… everything.

To my son Peter and sister Linda, who continue to be a great part of my life.

My Own Reflections II

by
Peter Vallas

A DREAM

I sit in awe as I watch her eyes,
someone special who says no lies.
She is warm and honest as can be,
and most of all she's dancing free.

Has faith put forth a change today,
I really don't know it's hard to say.
She's fun and loving and very sincere,
and I hope this change will better my year.

We danced together and enjoyed it much,
and I felt so good at her loving touch.
But time went by so fast it seems,
and now she remains in all my dreams.

You never know what may come of this,
I may not ever get a kiss.
But the friendship is the finest thing,
 for joy and happiness it will always bring.

A POEM ON THIS DREARY DAY

I write a poem on this dreary day,
To pass the time within,
My thoughts are long and far away,
And I realize now how long it's been.

Life has its ups and downs I guess,
But we must accept God's wish,
And there's just one point I'd like to stress,
That happiness and love is what I miss.

I hope someday that I shall overcome,
This feeling of despair,
For I miss him so my only son,
And I know he'll always be there.

What will happen in the years ahead,
When I am old and gray,
Will I be full of life or dead,
That is left for God to say.

I will love him no matter where I be,
In hell or heaven above,
As long as I have his memory,
And still remember his love.

A VALENTINE MESSAGE

Your fragrant smell,
the gleam in your eyes,
your soft touch,
the sweetness of your lips
your warm expressions

Beauty beyond compare,
thank you darling for all the love,
which you give so unselfishly,
thank you darling for your
compassion and understanding

Thank you darling for sharing
and thank you darling for being
MINE
I love you Rhoda,
always and forever,
Pete

ACCEPT THIS LIFE

To dream of wonderful things,
To love,
To sacrifice,
To die,
From beginning to end we must accept
     All that is written,
With love and happiness,
We don't question why,
But sadness and death,
     We say why?
There is no why,
This is our life
     To accept we must.
Carry on and seek out,
Love of life forever,
Be thankful for each
     Second, minute, hour,
For all that is given,
And thankful for just life and death,
     For it is our destiny.

ARE WE REAL

Are you real?
Do we know?
The many roles that are played in life.
        To conform with societies ideals,
but most important is what we are,
        the only role,
Which is our true self.
This we show by being honest,
but are we?
To expose our true feeling
our real selves.
NO,
But hide under the role of someone
        else,
then we have no identity,
but to survive we must.
Have our own self, identity,
because we are what we are,
we can change our roles,
but never change ourselves.
But that self satisfaction,
of being me.
For what I am
No one can challenge.

BAPTISM

Stillness lies along the beach,
Sunset closes in to mark the end of day
So peaceful,
Few people, walk the shore searching,
For the wonders of nature,
Yet further down appears a group,
Happy people
Among them a pretty girl, with
flowers, "Carol Jean."
Flowers show much love and faith.
But they are here to celebrate,
A part of life so saved,
A part of their faith.
She enters the water with joy,
her smile warm and soft.

Far out a ship passes,
Blinking its lonely light,
As a star in the sky

As a star in the sky
A short ways out her guidance unfolds,
And as she dipped below,
A new life is taken place.

The night life appears along the sand,
Even they come out to observe,
People watch as the cool breeze blows

Softly from the sea
The words are spoken and now
A return to shore
Unto the Christian faith
"Carol Jean"

Baptized as to God,
She follows as all those who have faith

BERNIE WHALEN

This man was made with love within,
Was gentle and kind to his friends and kin,
He had respect for the young and old,
It's a shame to let his story unfold.

He gave so much from his very heart,
And helped his girls to find a start,
It was March now and he loved the spring,
And when he awoke the birds would sing.

It's time to leave for work today,
And he looked at his wife as if to say,
What a beautiful day, my darling dear,
The spirit of spring is finally here.

He took his lunch and drove his car,
The way to work was not very far,
He drove around the winding bends,
And arrived at work to meet his friends.

He drank his coffee and ate his roll,
Not knowing today he would pay the toll,
Such a gorgeous day with a beautiful sky,
Who ever thought that he would die.

Away he goes so full of life,
Thinking of his lovely wife,
He didn't know he wouldn't come back,
But instead to perish along the track.

The time was just about 8:07,
When Bernie Whalen went to heaven,
Now he remains in God's loving care,
And his wonderful memories we have to share.

CHRISTMAS

The smell of evergreen,
　　　　　　Drifting through the house,
Carols sung throughout the town,
The odor of fresh pies and turkey,
People laughing and singing,
Love fills the air,
Little children sleep,
　　　　　　dreams of joy and happiness.
Parents wrapping gifts,
Lovers walking as the powdery snow
　　　　　　blows across their faces.
Such feelings at Christmas,
Sets the mood,
For the one tradition
　　　　　　which brings everyone closer.
Should every day be Christmas?

COME WITH ME

As I awoke one grizzly morn,
To start the day anew,
I was very glad that I was born,
And to fall in love with you.

You took your place within my life,
And made a man of me,
I want you for my wedded wife,
This faith was meant to be.

I know you are confused, my dear,
But try I must to prove,
That life is not all worry and fear,
And you must get on the move.

If you would try to break the tie,
And give to me your charms,
Then you will see it was not a lie,
And forever you'll be in my arms.

I know that you are really great,
And I wish you could see my way,
I hope you decide before it's too late,
If you'll come with me and stay.

CONFUSED

Don't be confused and act this way,
For we must continue day by day,
I know we all sometimes go astray,
But we can't be other than what we say.

Just look on life and do your part,
And give yourself a brand new start,
God sets your life upon his chart,
For you to follow by being smart.

There's nothing perfect today in life,
The world is full of all kinds of strife,
Fulfill your dream and become a wife,
To be loved and cherished the rest of your life.

DADDY

Daddy dear, I know you're near,
You've always been so nice,
You gave me all the love and cheer,
and passed on such good advice.

I miss you so all the time,
I never could forget,
How good you were and oh so kind,
And now I sit and fret.

Daddy dear, you were the one,
Who helped when things were tough,
So proud of me your only son,
You pulled me from the rough.

I sit alone and think of you,
Throughout the day and night,
You are one of the very few,
That would never, ever fight.

Now you're gone and I miss you so,
But your memory I hold,
I'll follow your steps until I go,
And the story will unfold.

DAISY

Snowy mountains,
Amidst the bright golden sun,
A refreshing pose,
Its stillness reflects upon such quite beauty,
       A sign of love,
       A sign of life,
Its green dress flowering in circles,
Many moods and life giving expressions,
So peaceful at rest,
Absence of cacophony,
Such pleasant thoughts to ease the mind,
A fragrance sweeter than perfume,
To feel as such can only bring to light,

The inner feeling of happiness,
       Of peace,
          Of love,
       Oh Daisy
You set my mind into a valley of youthful simplicity.

DEBBY

As the moonlight shines across the sea,
A vision of Debby came to be,
Her eyes were bright and full of love,
And they glittered as the starlight above.
She was warm and tender without a care,
But in her heart she wanted to share,
A love so full and from the heart,
A love so fine that I will never part.
Where is this love I wish to hold?
I've always wondered but was never told.
I hope someday I'll find my mate,
For a love like this is worth the wait.
I meant so much to fulfill my dream,
Without a care so peaceful and serene,
I never want to stand alone,
Just find what is written in the lines of this poem.

DECEMBER

The time has come again,
    this year,
For all the world to spread
    good cheer,
The thoughts of love fill
    the air,
And gifts galore for all
    to share,
Sharing is a very special thing
and only happiness can
    it bring,
Smile and be happy and
    try to remember,
And make every month
The month of December

DEPRESSED

When I feel empty and so very lost,
I try to be happy no matter the cost,
The ache inside can tear you apart,
So begin I must of a brand new start.

Depressed I am with nothing to say,
For it's very hard to find my way,
I search for many things to do,
And still I feel that I lost too.

I cry so hard all through the night,
And it leaves me with a terrible fright,
Of the things ahead that I must face,
But to do them right without disgrace.

But I must learn to follow through,
And someday I will fall in love too,
It's just that reason that keeps me alive,
For that life ahead I must really strive.

So whatever awaits me in the years to come,
I hope it's happy with lots of fun,
It's happiness I want to fulfill my life,
And to be loved and cherished with a wonderful wife.

DICK

I think of you so far away,
I wish that you would have chosen to stay,
You didn't have to be on top,
Only know when to stop.

I feel like you so many times
I even hear the church bells chime.
I thought the end would come tomorrow,
But I didn't want for my friend to sorrow.

To you, dear Sheila, was all heart
Right from the very start
You gave your love to family and kin,
And now we all know how long its' been.

You were a man of good and love,
And thanked God from high above,
Even though you made mistakes,
You gave it all, that's what it takes.

Because you wanted the best for them,
You felt you couldn't start again,
But I know how low you felt that day,
And I have only one thing to say.

You might not have made the best decision,
But your love was there deep within,
No matter what the future holds,
We'll always love you as life unfolds.

DISAPPOINTMENT

Today I met a lovely girl,
She was so pretty too,
Her eyes were fair just like a pearl,
I said, "Darling I'm in love with you."

We spoke awhile and share our talk,
As we strolled along the beach,
And as we finished our beautiful walk,
I began to make my speech.

"My fairest maiden most of all,
I want you for my wife,
You are so beautiful, striking and tall,
Stay with me for the rest of your life."

She looked at me with much despair,
As she took the things she carried.
"You really look as if you care,
But I'm sorry, I'm happily married!"

DOREEN

Throughout all my life I have never seen,
Such a wonderful girl as my Doreen.
She's true and honest without a care,
And a heart full of love for us to share.
She came one day from far away,
And I really hoped that she would stay,
For she's changed my life in a certain way,
And the things I feel I can hardly say.
We've known each other for just a short time,
And a girl like her is hard to find.
But there she was so full of love,
It's as if she was sent form the stars above.
She's warm and sweet with loving charms,
And I want to hold her in my arms.
To remember these days forever more,
Mean so much to me as never before.
But I know real soon I must face the fact,
She will have to leave and go on back,
I know it's hard for us to part,
But she'll always be within my heart.
We never know what lies ahead,
But return she might someday instead,
And bring with her that special gleam,
I'll always remember, in my darling Doreen.

DREAMS COME TRUE

I've always had this dream
      so real.
I've always known you,
      so beautiful,
I've always loved you,
      so close to me.

Yet to find you an almost impossible task,
a one in a million chance.
a never ending search for
a love so true.

I knew you,
I felt you,
I loved you.

In all my dreams
But who are you?
Where are you?
In my heart
In my mind.

And gods greatest gift of life
Rhoda
I found you
My dreams became a reality,
and now I can live and love,
all those beautiful thoughts.

DRUG DEATH

Death ebbs away slowly,
It waits
        prolongs,
So young yet she dies
        in agony,
So innocent with so much to live for,
The needle takes its toll,
The drug swiftly moves throughout the body,
Killing all life within,
But this is not the first
              nor the last
They can't live without
Yet to have is the beginning
               of the end.

DUTCHESS COUNTY

Oh, but what a wondrous dream,
To see the trees with leaves so green,
To watch them blowing to and fro,
And the leave's bright colors changing so.

It's just before the winter's snow,
When the autumn leaves put on their show,
It holds such beauty beyond compare,
A fluorescent picture for you to share.

The rolling hills and mountains high,
Are set upon the beautiful sky,
These beautiful settings upon the bounty,
You will find as you travel through Dutchess County.

ENDURING LOVE

The smell of country and morning dew,
Reminds me of the love I have for you,
You're as fresh as the air which flows on by,
And as cute as the angel in the sky.

You're kind and gentle all the time,
And sweet as honey as it may seem,
You're the kind of person that's hard to find,
You'll only find her in my dreams.

But a dream it is that you are here,
And there's nothing I can do,
But remember this time year by year,
And wonder if you loved me too?

Now I go my way and do my part,
Be it lonely or secure,
But I can't remove you from my heart,
For your love I must endure.

FAITH

Anxiety prevails,
    deep inside,
        hurt,
           disappointment.
But yet a challenge to survive.
Faith holds the greatest part,
Without it we fail,
To have it we must find ourselves,
        Lose our society-made roles,
Believe in one's self,
If honest, we become closer,
        to our own identity.
Then we can see God,
        within our soul.
He guides us through all life,
He gives us the inspiration to continue,
He gives us the faith and courage,
To make life the beautiful thing it is,
For without faith,
        without love,
        without God,
Our lives are empty and we have nothing.

FOG

What is this blanket from afar,
That keeps the sunshine away,
You can't even walk or drive a car,
And the children can't even play

Its fine mist which spreads so thin,
Settles all around the town,
Its wet and damp like it's always been,
And it makes you want to frown.

Oh go away you dreary fog,
Let the beauty of the sun come out,
We don't want to look at a darkened bog,
And we don't want to sit and pout.

But soon the heavens will open up,
And the sun comes shining through,
Across the street I see a pup,
And even he is happy too.

The town wakes up and the sky gets brighter,
And the fog is lifted afar,
The people smile as the day gets lighter,
As they leave their doors ajar.

Away with you, Oh dreary thing,
We need you not at all,
Darkness and trouble you always bring,
in winter, summer and even fall.

Well now you're gone and all is well,
We hope you never come back,
But only nature and time will tell,
You're something we'd rather lack.

FRIENDS

What are friends some people say?
They are those that treat you
in a special way,
To comfort you when things get bad,
and share your feelings
when happy or sad.

To help one another from beginning to end,
this is the one you can call your friend,
to love and cherish from each day on,
and to understand their feelings when
they are gone.

So a friend is more than just a person,
that is why you must be certain,
to have this trust is a special thing,
that honesty can only bring.

GODDESS OF LOVE

The beauty shines
Far across the land,
The inner feelings,
Of possession,
Love,
Everything is forgotten
Aphrodite beholds,
Without love there is
Nothing,
      To touch
      To hold
      To caress
      To feel,
So great is this part of life
Yet so necessary
      To live
For without love
We are deep within
The dungeons of hell,
But the reaching hand
Of the Goddess
Holds life together
      To continue
      To the hereafter

GONE AWAY

As the raindrops fall from beneath the sky,
I sit in my window and begin to cry,
Where is the love I'm longing for,
I think of her and want her more.

She left me a long, long time ago,
And never let me try and show,
The happiness and love I could give to her,
And I realize now how long its' been.

I tried so hard to forget the past,
And it seems like time has gone so fast,
They say I'll find my love someday,
So I take the time to kneel and pray.

If someday God returns her to me,
I will make her happy and let her see,
I'll be very happy to be her groom,
And she will always have the best things in life.

GOODBYE MY LOVE

Goodbye my love wherever you are,
I'll never forget you dear,
Whether you be near or far,
I'll feel as though you are here.

The fun we had, the times we laughed,
Are gone forever more,
I hate to say it all has passed,
And we must close the door.

Life wasn't easy all the time,
And there was sorrow and strife,
But more than anything you were mine,
And I was glad you were my wife.

We were together for so long
It was like an eternity,
My love for you is oh so strong,
As you were a part of me.

In my heart you will always be,
My guiding light above,
You'll always be in my memory,
And I'll never forget your love.

So goodbye my love forever more,
Now you're in God's best of care,
I'll still love you as before,
And someday I'll meet you there.

HAPPY BIRTHDAY

Happy birthday Rhoda, my dream,
The most beautiful girl I've ever seen,
Just holding you in my very arms,
Fills me with love and all your charms.

Be happy my dear, is all I say,
Because this is your special day,
I wish you love from within my heart,
That you will give your life a start.

A life of happiness and love for you,
And I hope that I can share that too,
I offer you my heart and soul,
To be together as we grow old.

I want you to know that I truly care,
And you know that I will always be there,
I know that I'm within your life,
And pretty soon you'll be my wife.

So God bless you dear, for ever more,
And for you Rhoda, I open the door,
That you have the happiness that you seek,
And forever and ever it will keep.

HISTORY IS LIFE AND DEATH

I have been here
Before?
Yes,
Through the ages,
before and after
The rebirth of history
holds deep within.
Birth the beginning of the end.
What end?
Death a continuation of Life
the hereafter or the here before
in this life as all life,
I read history.
But all is a collection
of thoughts
I have been there
I made history.
To die is to live again
What will I be?
I feel what I was
I know
Life and Death is history
repeating itself
through ages and ages, forever.

HONESTY

Do we face what things in life we must accept?
We cover its meaning,
                    What life is.
We are blessed to follow the cause,
                    set by God.
But we improvise,
                    the very structure of life itself,
We mask the truth, we cover our identity,
                    to be not,
                              ourselves.
But something we are not...
                    Can't we be honest?
To be honest may expose what we really are,
But what are we?

We will never know,
                    be honest
                    be me
                         be you.

For no matter how we hide,
                    the truth unfolds,
                              when we answer
                                   to our maker.

Why only in time of distress, we call on God?
    Why not call on God every day?
        Unleash the secrets of life,
            Release from the soul its troubles,
                Receive piece of mind, and be yourself,
                    For we can't hide what we really are.

I GAVE

She wanted love,
        I gave.
She wanted trust,
        I trusted.
She wanted compassion,
        I gave compassion,
She wanted child,
        I gave child.
She left,
No more to see,
But why?
I forgive
        as God forgave.
I cried the tears of life,
I asked for reasons,

Oh God bring forth
        and give strength.
Did I forsake He,
        Who giveth life?
Yet how or when?
        Suffer I must as God.
Happiness will prevail,
        Someday.
I wait for the time,
Release the ache from within,
        time and hope and faith,
I shall have again,
        Ecstasy.

I LOVE YOU WITH ALL MY HEART

I love you dear with all my heart,
Believe in me if you will,
And may we never drift apart,
For our dreams we must fulfill.

A life of happiness lies ahead,
As our troubles drift away,
And in our minds we will imbed,
The love we have for each other today.

Faith played its part within our lives,
To bring us close together,
And soon you'll be one of many wives,
Whose love will last forever.

I love you dear with all my heart,
So deep, so lovely, so true,
Only you can give me a start,
And prove I will, that I love you.

I MISS YOU SO

I miss you so
It was just like yesterday
But time has gone
And I feel so sad.

I want you dear,
And I hope you'll understand me,

The time has come,
For you to decide
I'll love you always.

Just give me a chance
And you will see
I'll be your man
And set you free.

So please don't ever go,
Come stay with me,
You know I miss you so.

I THINK OF YOU

Whenever I am alone,
I think of you.
Whenever I am far away,
I think of you.
Whenever I am depressed,
I think of you.
Whenever I am lonely,
I think of you.
Whenever I am thankful,
I think of you.
Whenever I think of life,
I think of you.
Whenever I think of having it all,
It is you . . . . .

JAIL

It's been such a long time,
and I'm thin and pale,
I wonder if they'll be so kind,
to release me from this jail.

I made a mistake and it's taken from me,
ten years of my life in this rotten cell,
I wish I knew when it would be,
my release from this awful, lonely hell.

I thought that I was going soon,
but something stood in the way,
Yet here I am sitting in the gloom,
as I wait each and every day.

I know I must pay for that awful day,
when I took that poor man's life,
But it wasn't supposed to happen that way,
and widowed his wonderful wife.

Now I know what life is about,
and I hope someday to find,
It does no good to sit and pout,
for I'll never have peace of mind.

JOHN CALDES

He came here many years ago,
To start his life anew,
He wanted nothing better to show,
He was one of the chosen few.

He could work his way up to the top,
And have everything to give,
He'd always work and never stop,
For he really wanted to live.

His children loved him ever so much,
And he gave to them his love,
He catered to their loving touch,
And he thanked the Lord above.

Along the way he had some trouble,
No one can ever foresee,
And his dream had burst just like a bubble,
No one can say; it was meant to be.

He served the church whenever he could,
And loved his family and kin,
He treated people as he should,
And realized now how alone he's been.

He helped many people along the way,
And was sharp, intelligent and coy,
He was loved by all, each and everyday,
And his love was all for "JOY".

H never wanted sympathy and pity,
He wanted to fulfill his dream,
For he loved his darling sister Kitty,
For as long as it may seem.

Now God has taken this wonderful man,
High above the sea,
And his goodness remembered across the land,
A beautiful person, John Caldes.

KIM

I cannot think how long it's been,
Nor remember at any time,
A sweet little girl by the name of Kim,
Just as cute as you can find.

She runs along the drifting sand,
The wind blowing through her hair,
And she holds her brother by the hand,
So free and pure without a care.

So pretty is she with life ahead,
And with a guiding hand above,
She'll leave the grief and go instead,
To a life of happiness and love.

LIFE

I have been here before
                    Yes,
Through the ages,
Before and after,
The rebirth of history
                    Holds deep within,
Birth the beginning of the end?
What end?
Death a continuation of life
                    the hereafter or the here before.
In this life as all life
I read history
But all is a collection of thoughts
I have been there;
I made history.
To die is to live again,
What will I be?
I feel what I was,
                    I know,
Life and death is history,
                    repeating itself
                    through ages and ages
                                        forever.
The answers have been found
But mankind will not face
                    What is in the eye of the beholder
He fills his thoughts with questions
                    and translates false truths to cover
                    what is really in his heart.
As one good book says,
        I AM THE RESURRECTION AND THE LIFE."
And it speaks for all
But aren't we also the resurrection and the life?

LIFEGUARD

Yes he watches the sea today
as he does each and everyday,
To protect our lives from
the angry sea,
He sits and watches you and me.

When someone's in trouble
He jumps off his chair
and we all thank God that
he is there,
He saves our life forever
more
He's our protector upon the
shore.

LIFE'S WHEEL

In life we are all part of a wheel,
Revolving around slowly,
Each spoke is a trail to our destiny,
It turns around as our life does,
If the wheel is unshaped,
So are our lives,
But if the wheel is balanced,
Our lives are smooth.

It may have its bumps and grinds,
But if taken care of it smoothes out,
Sometimes we are on the bad road,
Sometimes on the good road.
But to guide this wheel along,
The road which is best,
Will provide a longer lasting life,
                    of easy riding.

LINDA

Linda, Linda I love you so,

Please don't ever let me go.

People say who is she?

She's a doll who is sister to me.

She's full of life with lots of love;

Sometimes she sings like the angels above,

I love her so and she is so nice,

Just like a cookie of sugar and spice.

LIVING THINGS

Such living things,
the smell
the touch
the sounds

All beautiful in my mind,
exquisite of life and nature,
its excellence arouses,
such feelings,
never to explain
for real
imagine yes,
but to see,
only through the mind.

For I lack the most precious gift
thy sight,
and my most desire
to see
such living things.

LOVE

The beauty shines

                    far across the land,
The inner feelings of passion

                    of love
Everything is forgotten,

                    Aphrodite beholds,
Without love there is nothing.
To touch

          to hold

            to feel,

So great is this part of life
Yet so necessary

             to live

              to express
For without love
We are deep within

                    the dungeons of hell
But the far reaching hand of the Goddess,
Holds life together

             to continue

              to the hereafter.

LOVE OF LIFE

As I walk among trees so big and green,
There was so much beauty as I've never seen,
The flowers bloom among the ground cover,
For they are there to inspire a lover,
Climbing above the branches high,
I saw something move against the sky,
It was a baby and mother raccoon,
Their reflection was set against the moon.
As darkness set they disappeared from view,
And I knew right then life is like that too,
For just a while upon the earth are we,
And then without warning wére in eternity

MARIE

As I walked along the ocean side,
My thoughts were deep within,
So sad I was and how I cried,
So lonely it has been.

I looked across the beautiful pool,
And much to my surprise,
I saw a girl so refreshingly cool,
With lots of love in her eyes.

Our eyes had met with a quickened glance,
My heart began to beat,
I knew that I didn't have a chance,
For she swept me off my feet.

She was so pretty and lovely too,
So sweet with warm delight,
A heart so pure and very true,
Like an angel in her flight.

We found each other this special day,
And I was happy that I did see,
Such a wonderful girl, who came my way,
My darling sweet, Marie.

MARY ANN

This angel came from up above,
She was full of life and so much love,
She wasn't big or even tall,
Just a little girl, sweet and small.

She touched my heart in a certain way,
I can't even find the words to say,
She belonged to someone at this time,
But a nicer girl you couldn't find.

An inspiration in this great life,
She'll make some guy a wonderful wife,
For just a short time she was in view,
People like this, there are but few.

Now she's gone on her way,
And I'll never forget her smile today,
As I sit here writing on the sand,
I think of that lovely Mary Ann.

MIGHTY OCEAN

The thunder of waves
Their crushing blows
Foams never ending climb
The sounds increase
                    as a thousand drums roll.

But yet a sound of peace
As man it gets angry
                    It gives life
                    It gives death
                    It gives joy
                    It gives terror
Many moods does it possess
                    as we possess

But respect we must show
For its mighty power
Unleashes the strength of many Gods
And speak it does
Its message clear
It's been there
                    since the existence of the world
And no fool lies within.

MISSING YOU

Even though you're away,
It's so nice to have someone to miss,
To miss you brings you closer,
    I can smile.
Thoughts of you are happy,
Thoughts of you are warm,
And as time passes on,
That special feeling grows,
And when you return,
My heart bursts with gladness,
It's been so nice missing you.

MOTHER

She was always good and kind at heart,
Even from the very start,
She gave so much throughout the years,
Keeping us happy and removing our fears.

She was there when needed all the time,
A wonderful person you'll never find,
She had a beautiful heart of gold,
Even now as she is getting old.

Our trust in her was always there,
And many good times we all did share,
There could never be a person other,
Than our one and only beautiful mother.

MY CHOICE MY RHODA

If I were given a choice,
to have anything in the world.
What would I choose?

If I could have all the gold,
If I could have all the diamonds,
If I could have all the money.

I would choose you.
You are all the things that,
Money
Gold
Diamonds
could never buy.

MY DARLING WIFE

If ever I am alone
       I think of you.
If ever I am far away
       I think of you.
If ever I am depressed
       I think of you.
If ever I am lonely
       I think of you
If ever I am thankful
       I think of you.
If ever I think of life
       I think of you.
If ever I think of having it all
       It is you.

MY LOVE

As I stepped into the door of my plane,
I looked back and saw her pretty face,
I didn't know if it was the raindrops,
      or the tears running down my face.
My love,
To be left behind in her world of uncertainty,
I will travel many miles away,
To my world of loneliness and hunger for that very love,
Will we ever see each other again?
A constant thought,
This ache within me to carry each day,
May the truth within ourselves bring us closer,
So we may want each other forever.

MY LOVE AWAITS

The wind howls across the vastness of the fields,
Dark clouds cast a shadow below,
The icy cold works its way through my body so,
     Pain, shiver,
Ahead lies the warmth of home a few miles,
I survive this walk through winter's scorn,
For my love awaits,

     and as I approach,
The smell of hot apple pie,
     the chestnuts roasting,
To pick up my snifter of full-bodies rum,
As it flows through, it fires my body next to the
     crackle of flames of the fireplace.
I lie back in her arms,
     and our bodies come together,
     sweat flows,
     lips meet,
Ah, but the love of life,
     excretes with passion,
I unleash a never-ending surge of love,
Yes, I walk these miles each day,
     for all its worth,
     this love for which I hold.

MY SON

A most glorious day appeared in my life,
The day a son was born to me and my wife,
I was so happy and full of thrills,
As I stood there watching him in his buttons and frills.

A few months later, as I watched him play,
I began to think of that wonderful day,
When he was born upon this earth,
I thanked God for his blessed birth.

And as each day passed he grew and grew,
And he played with me as if he knew,
I'm glad you are my father dear,
And I'll love you more year by year.

I cherished him with all my pride,
And I hoped he would always be at my side.
But then one day he went away,
When I had thought that he would stay,
I prayed to God for his return,
And hoped someday that I would learn,
The reason for this ungrateful thing.

I see him once now every week,
And when I do I can hardly speak
As the tears fall and the years go by,
My love for him will never die,
But I keep abreast and hope in fact,
That someday, somehow, he will come back.

MY UNITED STATES

So proud I am,
                It's mine,
                        It's free,
I can say what I want,
                Express myself,
Plot my course of life.
It's mine,
                        Yes,
How wonderful to live in peace,
In a land untouched by the scars of war,
Thank you people all over the world,
        who gave their lives,
                So I may have all this.
Yes, thank you,
                For it's mine,
                        My country.
So great,
                This United States.

Dedicated, January 20, 1981, to the 53 former American Hostages

NATURE

I hear the winds blowing softly through the trees,
I feel the leaves falling gently in the breeze,
The sun is warm and shining bright,
The birds are gliding above,
Their beauty reflects along their flight,
I feel the meaning of love

I walk the forest huge and green,
It beholds such beauty I've never seen,
The squirrels climb the trees so high,
They cast a shadow against the sky

The sunlight gleams from high above,
And it casts a feeling of happiness and love,
The water trickles down the stream,
And the fish are swimming smart and clean.

Its' cool, refreshing, oh what a view,
And I feel I want to start anew,
I sit in awe my mind at rest,
I'm seeing nature at its best

Oh thank you God that nature be,
So beautiful in its stride,
It makes the world feel so free,
And I'm glad to be alive

NEW CHRISTMAS

Pretty lights you flicker so,
And reflect such colors in the snow.
I wait all year for Christmas time,
To watch the trees and see them shine.

So much love and so much cheer,
Should be spread throughout the year.
Why wait for the lovely month of December,
For Christmas time so you can remember.

Love and peace to carry on,
Hate and despair will now be gone,
Peace on earth forever more,
Let's spread our love from door to door.

NEW FRIEND

I sit in awe as I watch her eyes,
Someone special who says no lies,
She's warm and honest as can be,
And most of all she's dancing free.

Has faith put forth a change today,
I really don't know it's hard to say,
She's fun and loving and very sincere,
And I hope this change will better my year.

We danced together and enjoyed it much,
And I felt so good at her loving touch,
But time went by so fast it seems,
And now she remains in all my dreams.

You never know what may come of this,
I may never even get a kiss,
But the friendship is the finest thing,
For joy and happiness it will always bring.

NOWHERE

Did you ever ask yourself what nowhere is?
It's a place where people go when
                they can't think straight,
If they turn right, there is nothing,
If they turn left, there is nothing,
If they go up, there is nothing,
If they go down, there is nothing.

How did they get there?

By not taking life for what it really is.
By not living in reality,
By not being honest with themselves.

Nowhere, Nowhere,
                the cry of so many,
How unfortunate for those whose minds
                lead them astray.
Well balanced thoughts can only solve this
                mystery of life.
Take today for what it is and be happy for today.
Yesterday is gone and can solve nothing
                in today's world.
Tomorrow is the result of a good today.

No tomorrow is the result of being nowhere…

OCEAN

The thunder of the waves,
their crushing blow.
Foams never ending climb,
the sounds increase as
a thousand drums roll
But yet a sound of peace
as now it gets angry.
It gives life,
It gives death,
It gives joy,
It gives terror.
Many moods does it possess
as we possess.
But respect we must show,
For its mighty power
unleashes.
The strength of many Gods
and speak it does
its message clear
always and forever.

PEOPLE

The reason for mankind's existence,
For without them there is none,
What are they?

>Persons,
>>Yes,

What do we see?
Some people say:

>They're Jews,
>They're Italians,
>They're Catholics,
>They're Blacks,
>They're Indian.

But aren't they all the same?
I see people,
Bodies all the same,

>legs, arms, hearts,

Together we make up the structure of life,
Together to share peace on earth,
We all belong.

But the minds are different,

>so sad,

We all feel the same things,

>hurt
>love
>death
>joy

What makes us different?

>We are not.

For we all are people,
And together we make up this beautiful world

>in which we live.

PLAY ON LIFE

Many faces appear in the night life,
The expression of one's self,
Searching,
>for that dream in the sky,
>>a play,
>>>a character,
>>>>a role.

The mystic change within,
Self satisfaction of the soul,
>deep within a feeling,
An expression of faith,
The unknown challenge of life,
Many minds,
>many thoughts,
>>many feelings,
The thoughts of so many set the stage,
And unfold an act,
>>>uncomfortable,
>>>>strange.

I watch this play,
I see the tears,
>>no applause,
I am but an audience of one,
My theater,
>my play,
>>my character,
All focused into one.
I applaud what is real,
>>ME.

RHODA MY LOVE

I've waited for so many years,
To share this special moment,
With someone I love,
You're here Rhoda,
And I love you,
Please love me,
And I will love you forever,
To be at each other's side,
To comfort each other,
A dream in my world,
A never ending feeling of love,
      Of passion,
         Of truth,
            Of Happiness.

You Rhoda, are my dream,
You Rhoda I want,
You Rhoda I love,
Give me a chance,
So I may find me,
And together we will live.

SAILING

The dawn broke through, away went the night
The birds are winging along in their flight
Streams of sunlight shine with care
And the warmth of April fills the air.

Down to the dock I make my way
To sail my boat on this beautiful day
I packed my lunch and bottle of wine
And now to launch this boat of mine.

We slip through the water of darkened blue
And the salty mist is spraying me too
I look at the water moving to and fro
It's like a thousand lights shining below.

What beauty is cast along the way
And I thank the Lord for this perfect day
I will sail along until September
With most beautiful memories, I'll always remember.

SCOTT

What friend I have that means a lot?
A wonderful boy by the name of Scott.
He makes me happy when I'm with he,
And I hope forever, my friend he'll be.

He lives so far, far away,
Yet thoughts of him will brighten my day,
Good times together we did see,
And good memories they will always be.

And I hope some day things will get better,
So we can spend more time together,
For me, for you, and your mother Doreen,
Let us all be together like a wondrous dream.

SO LOVELY SO TRUE

Once when I was lonely and blue,
I met a girl so lovely and true,
Her eyes sparkled like crystal glass,
And at that moment I forgot the past.
She was like a flower in the beauty of its bloom,
And I hoped to see her again real soon.
I no longer thought of trouble and strife,
The day Rhoda came into my life.
She was so gay and full of fun,
I began to feel as if we were one,
I never thought happiness would come my way,
And now more than ever I wanted it to stay.
Her smile was warm and free as the air,
And her charms were soft without a care,
Her lips were sweet and full of love,
And she glittered like the starlight above,
I hope this happiness will continue in our heart,
And may we never drift apart,
But continue on from year to year,
I thank you Rhoda for being such a dear.

STACEY

Splashing through the water so cool and clean,
The cutest girl I've ever seen,
The carefree way she swims along,
So dancing free and full of song.

Remember when we felt this way,
It seems like it was just yesterday,
Happy and young from the very start,
With all the love within our heart.

So light as a butterfly gliding above,
She moves along so full of love,
Her pretty eyes how they shine so,
As two little stars, oh how they glow.

So little Stacey, keep in mind,
You're simply one of a special kind,
To remain as happy as you are today,
I'll pray for you each and everyday.

STEPHANIE

Oh little girl, you are like a flower
As I watch you play upon this hour
You dance so lovely and oh so strong
Graceful in motion, piercing in song.

Your eyes are wide and shining bright
Its gleam is like a glowing light
And as you run along the sand
You shine within the beautiful land.

Mommy watches as she's always known
As you lie asleep midst the warmth of home
You're everything for which I care
And you hold that beauty beyond compare.

The stars soon appear out of the night
You're such a peaceful and loving sight
As the clouds pass over so dark and blue
With such fluorescence of life so true.

May your life be like a wondrous dream
And you'll be so happy, joyous and serene
God will watch over and let you be
The sweetest girl in the world, my Stephanie.

STRENGTH IN LIFE

Sometimes I wonder
I give all my love
Just to be happy
Just to be loved
Love is so special
  The sharing
The understanding
But the insecurities in life
Can threaten its beauty
And drive you further into unhappy
  Thoughts
But the power of the mind can filter its
  Impurities
How strong one can be to think for both
To tighten all the strings that bind life
  Itself
To leave no loose ends
To complete the package of life
Is never an easy task

SUCH BEAUTY

The spring thaw sets in,
Clear water trickling down the brook,
The golden sun shining from the east,
A treasure of life so beautiful,
     So cool,
          So refreshing,
Spring flowers blooming along the bank,
Tadpoles swimming in the clear,
A lonely frog sunning itself,
The sound of water flowing over pebbles,
They cast a reflection of colorful stones,
As a rainbow creeps across the valley,
A prism with a million lights.

TAKEN AWAY

The wind blowing gently across the sand,
Oh, but beauty far and vast,
The trees rise along the shoreline,
How peaceful
It was only a few years,
        but man came,
            destruction of nature.
Tall buildings rise high above,
The once pure beaches now clutter with debris,
The sand no longer white but gray with filth,
The air filled with smog,
        no more landscape,
        no more seascape,
Man calls it beauty,
I call it destruction,
The once blue skies now,
        clouded with mist,
The once clear waters,
        black with oil.
God gave all this for us to enjoy,
Yet we take away the beauty of nature.
What will this writer find in years to come?
A concrete world,
        pills,
        machines,
Our lives will then be mechanical,
With no beauty,
Self-destruction and greed,
        for man is really selfish.

THE BEST THINGS IN LIFE

The wheat fields shine golden in the breeze,
And a soft wind is blowing through the trees,
The tractor moves slowly across the field,
The beauty is such that I must yield.

I walk across the grassy knoll,
And watch all these beautiful things,
This land I hope is never sold,
For the best things in life it brings.

THE GARDEN OF EARTH

The earth is like a garden,
mixed with many plants,
      the fruits of life,
      who shall survive.

Those who grow with each days challenges,
those who desire to live on,
those who absorb the good,
those who remain strong, and weather the furies of life.

The desire to live,
      only the weak shall fall,
      and some of those who fall,
may survive,
but with strong will and sound mind.
Those plants shall flourish forever.
Are we so much like this?

THE GREEK

Across the treacherous paths
     he leads his sheep,
to pastures on the mountain side,
watching and herding along,
       as day break comes he travels home.

The small Ionian Village lies below
     in the valley,
he breaks bread with wine and cheese,
he dances to the Bouzouki music,
      happy with life so simple.

     Yes
families join together
        To feast
        To dance
Lambs roast over the open fire,
       Happy people
For the most important thing in life,
       is happiness.

THE HERO

Flames run high
        heat intense
Smoke so thick
    Blind
Babies cry
Save the children
Must sacrifice, sweat, blood, tears, pain
Duty to mankind
        Muscles ache, torture
But here we arrive
Now to release from death to
        protect
Effort untold but realistic
        to survive
        safe at last
Spared again to live
        danger forever, but yes
Bravery beyond compare
        the giver of life
Like God, with so much respect
        give thanks
Life goes on to repeat again
        until no more he reigns
The price will always be paid
But to continue playing the part
        for the good of mankind.

THE KEY

I'll always love you as today,
No matter what may be,
I know there's not much for me to say,
For I must wait until you're free.

I wanted to have the only key,
Right from the very start,
So someday you would only say to me,
Come darling and open my heart.

But I will wait for that special day,
The rest of my life if I must,
Of those special words I want you to say,
Here's my love, my life, and my trust.

THE KINGDOM BELOW

As I dive beneath the cool waters,
a sight of untold beauty.
a different world,
       quite serene,
a beauty never before seen,
suspended below.
Thousands of years of history,
fish swimming along,
as if in space,
silence beholds.
Only through their eyes do they speak,
un-disturbed in their habitat,
each day they move and feed.
A special watch,
       to survive
but that unknown predator,
can take away.
but necessary for the survival,
of this beautiful kingdom.

THE LOVE THAT BURNS INSIDE

What is this love that burns inside?
Why does it hurt so much?
It can destroy all your pride,
And leave your heart empty at its touch.

I feel as though I'm far apart,
And depressed and sad as can be,
How do you mend a broken heart,
And rid the tears to see?

Well listen my brother, to good advice,
You must not break apart,
You're bound to meet someone nice,
And have a brand new start.

These things will happen once in a while,
Don't sulk with guilt or shame,
You're only acting like a child,
And it's not for you to blame.

It's over now so look ahead,
And look for the love that waits,
Take this day your daily bread,
That's what the good book states.

So forget the past which is behind,
And pray to the Lord above,
By keeping faith you will always find,
That everlasting love.

THE SEA

As I look across the beautiful sea,
Such beautiful blue skies,
In contrast to the
    Blue green waters,
A reflection of peaceful soft
    colors,
An artists dream,
Sets the mood,
The only change
The eyes of those who see,
    Yet, for hundreds of years,
This sight to behold,
By those who are forgotten today.
As they stood in the
    Crystal clear water,
The gems of the ocean floor,
Shining through with such
    Magnificence,
The mind mellows with beautiful
    thoughts,
The sound of the waves,
An orchestra playing in
the background,
The ripple of the tide,
Carrying a never ending
Waltz.
For the sea is like a large
Book,
With stories of history, love, war,
Peace,
Which will be read
Forever.

THE STAR ABOVE

I see a star so far away
It seems as though it has something to say,
Speak my star from high above,
Tell me there is someone to love.

I fill my dreams with such beautiful things,
And hope they come true with all it brings,
The twinkle of light, how it shines above,
Always gives me the feeling of a special love.

So far away in the galaxy of light,
It makes me feel good every night.

THE UNSUNG HEROES

The unsung heroes, who are they?
Who risk their lives every day,
They go unnoticed, without a care,
But if you need them, they're always there.

In day or night, in all kinds of weather,
They arrive at the scene and begin together,
A job that may not bring them home,
And leave their families all alone.

As they enter through the smoke and flames,
No one knows the many names,
Of the men who give without despair,
And risk their lives without a care.

But even though they may lose their life,
And leave their children and their wife,
They continue on each and every day,
With no recognition and little to say.

Who are these men who give so much,
And save many lives with their finer touch,
They are the men who break their backs,
The Firefighters of the City of Hackensack.

THIS WONDERFUL GLORIOUS DAY

On this wonderful and glorious day,
I am very glad to see,
My friends have been joined in a sacred way,
It was their faith to be.

As the tears drop and years go by,
There may be troubles and sorrow,
But their love for each other will never die,
Because there is always, tomorrow.

Side by side, they will make their way,
And keep their faith in each other,
For there will come that special day,
When they will be, father and mother.

They're happy now and much in love,
Look at their eyes how they shine,
They sparkle like the stars above,
And bless the happiness that they will find.

Well, now to you the bride and groom,
I wish you well with your plan,
And as you walk beneath the moon,
God be with you, forever,
Donald and Jo Ann.

TO DIE

As I sit and watch across the Keys
I feel a tingle in the breeze,
Its time for me to leave this world,
And leave my friends and my only girl.

Please don't let me face the fact,
That I may go and never come back,
I know dear God I must comply,
For we all must live and we all must die.

TO JOHN LENNON

This world today
        in flaming toil,
Upset together as if in a
        barrel mixed with hate.
Yes, those four things,
        if every man would do.
It's been said many years afore,
Don't act with confusion,
Love your fellow man,
Act with honest motives.

If mankind met with these ideals,
What a better world for us to live.
I listen to you, dear sir,
        a philosophy from the heart,
What does no good
        but yet
My soul is clear
        for love of my fellow man
But a preacher I am not
        to try I will
Sacrifice,
Bring love to the world,
Let man be guided,
The never ending struggle for peace,
Only through people being themselves,
        can we achieve this goal.
You tried with songs and expressions,
I tried with inspirations and
        my own reflections,
But lost amidst the greed of mankind,
People wake up...
Self destruction
        is imminent.

TO LOVE AGAIN

My heart is reaching out,
   Such pain,
   Yet full of love,
Where am I?
Who am I?
I want so much to love,
I want so much to be loved,
Will I really know?

I feel it,
   I am not afraid,
But I ask for that everlasting love,
That will grow forever,
Yet to face the uncertainty,
Which I have faced before,
And to be alone again,
No more could I live,
Death would be a welcomed sign,
But I must not give in,
I want to live,
I want to love,
And I will go on,
For I will not lose.

And give all I feel,
If it's God's will that I should lose again,
Then I will accept his wish,
And thank him for at least letting me love again.

TO SEE

Such living things
         the smell
               the touch
                     the sounds,
all beautiful in my mind,
exquisite of life and nature,
its excellence arouses
               such feelings,
never to explain
         for real
imagine
            yes
but to see,
         only through the mind,
for I lack the most precious gift
and my most desire
         to see such living things.

TOGETHER FOREVER

As each day passes,
I long for you more and more,
A feeling so deep,
Thinking of you,
        Makes me smile.
Seeing you,
        Makes me flutter,
Touching you,
        Makes me fill with passion.
You,
    And only you alone,
        Could possess such beauty,
If we feel together,
We could only melt,
        Into each other's hearts forever.

TRUE LOVE

I would give everything for you,
I would sacrifice all for you,
Because you are me,
And together we will find,
What everyone else is looking for,
A true love.

UNITED WAY

I couldn't talk,
I couldn't walk,
My life was filled with pain,
I was so sad,
    even mad,
For no sunshine, only rain.

I laid on my back,
Life was so black,
And I hoped for a brighter day,
    I stuck it out,
Then hear a shout,
Here comes the United Way.

UNITED WAY

For all those people who suffer in life,
With all their troubles, sorrow and strife,
They would never have a happy day,
If it weren't for the United Way.

Let's leave these people without a care,
And everyone give his fair share,
To those who need it most of all,
Then we can stand so proud and tall.

We may be healthy and very strong,
But what about those who can't move along,
Let's give them life and let us pray,
And thank God for the United Way.

UNKNOWN

Deep blue
Dark green
What contrast above and below
                they meet
                amidst sails
                far away
Horizon the farthest point
Infinity
Beyond what eternity
Seek out long lost secrets
Above and beyond or so deep
                as a dungeon
                to find the existence of the
                UNKNOWN

UNTITLED

Yet in times of stress,
We fall apart,
    The fault,
        The blame,
Yes, look upon yourself,
What purpose in life you bear,
We set upon our own goals,
    To wit,
        Oh, all is said,
We seek now,
    instead of before,
Understand for now,
Look for that purpose,
There is no blame,
For the gift of life is there,
To follow just ideals,
    the simple way,
Why face regrettable toil,
When you have the gift to decide,
What the future may bring.

UNTITLED

Such great distance between our lives,
But closeness,
                    Bodies together,
No,
But minds together,
Yes,
Dreams to fulfill,
                    The hope,
Together in mind,
A connection between souls,
Never ending thoughtfulness,
Feeling from within,
                    Preserve our love,
What no man can destroy,
A love from deep within,
                    True feelings,
                    Expression,
A never ending chain of thought,
Secures the bond,
                    Of true feelings,
To provide the necessary love in life.

UNTITLED

Love is all the things I see in you,
   Beauty,
      Life,
         Feelings,
            Compassion.
All the things I want so desperately,
Yet I feel you are still,
      so far away,
Are you ready for me?
Confused
      maybe,
You love me,
   Yes,
But a desire to hold such independence,
Sharing must be complete,
         A total feeling of all,
But what is best for you,
      is what counts,
You must know for sure,
        for life must not be wasted.
Sometimes time answers this question,
Yet sometimes time takes its toll.
Give of all those feelings,
      to that one person,
Who can give all of himself,
And if it's not possible,
Then don't hold life in your hands,
Which you don't know what to do with.

UNTITLED

As I run my fingers through your hair,
A world of excitement opens up,
Your touch,
    So warm,
        So tender,
            Your lips so soft.
Ecstasy, what every person longs for,
But only two special people,
With feelings the same,
Can experience such pleasure.

UNTITLED

God give me strength,
To hold onto this life,
To keep this love forever.
Give her the strength,
To discover her true feelings,
of life itself.
Clear away the cobwebs,
Which cloud her head,
Open up the vaults of happiness,
And spread the mist of love.
Give us direction,
So we may find each other,
Make our paths cross,
So we may take the last road together.

UNTITLED

The answers have been found
But mankind will not face,
What is in the eye
      of the beholder.
He fills his thoughts with
      Questions
And translates false truths
to cover what is really
in his heart.

As the Lord said,
I am the resurrection and the
Life,
and he speaks for all
But aren't we also the
Resurrection and the Life?

UN-TITLED

the sun burst

like a flower
    a bloom
    a child

rose petal

life's beginning of each
but then to nature be thy faith
decides whom shall survive

WHAT IS DESTRUCTIVE

He said come
        he came

The thunder but resurrection
bent upon some plunder
        Life Death
                to giveth all
        love cherish
                Man
But how faith has no part
                in each
Falsehood holds
The mouth speaks
                        DESTRUCTIVE
Worse than all
To recover...Maybe
                        with honesty
                        with truth
                        with love
                        with faith
Love of Life
                        to carry
Must bring untold truths
Feelings
                        desperation
                            to begin
                                to end
Eternity.

WHAT IS LIFE

LIFE IS UNDERSTANDING
LIFE IS GIVING
LIFE IS ACCEPTING
LIFE IS SHARING
LIFE IS PEACE
LIFE IS LOVE
WHAT ELSE COULD ANYONE WANT?

WHERE AM I

Why is that I must always be
So blind that I can never see
That a puppet am I that people use
I always try but always lose.

I want to be happy and ever so free,
But I must be myself or it's not me
I try very hard to do the right thing
And when I'm down I always sing.

I want to forget the past in my life,
And become somebody's wonderful spouse,
To be loved and cherished forever more
And then on this story I can close the door.

God give me help which I do need
And give me the power and I will heed
To open my heart to the greatest girl
And love her forever and that's no lie.

WHERE ARE YOU

Where are you my love?
I'm thinking of you
          as always,
I hope you are thinking of me,
What better thoughts could we have,
Than of each other.
But if your thoughts are not
          with me now,
And if you choose to share
          with someone else,
I won't think bad thoughts,
          for it is your choice.
Your eyes will tell,
Will your mind speak out,
          in total truthfulness?
Or will you mask sharing this with one who loves you.
If you love me only the truth can speak out,
And I'll love you more,
Honesty can only bring us closer.

WHITE STALLION

A flash of white crosses
the prairie,
Dust filters across the
dry land,
A mirage or is it really
there,
The white stallion
running free,
full of life
but yet
Its' beauty flashes
across the sky,
I want him
      now
but so have others
yet free he remains
to roam,
In his free world
forever.

WHO SURVIVES

The sun burst

        like a flower
        a bloom
        a child

Rose petal

        life's beginning of each
        but then to nature by thy faith
        decides whom shall survive.

WHY ME

Where is everything?
I see clouds.
What time is it?
Where am I?
So much trouble,
So much pain,
Why must I loose
the most important thing to me?
Why must I suffer such torment?
Why…
My self respect,
My love,
My feelings,
My beliefs,
all so very important.
But most of all
I can accept all the clouds.
The pain,
The trouble,
and I will not loose.
I love life,
I want life,
I have life.
And no one can ever take away
the most important thing,
which means so much to all
ME

YOU ARE LIFE

Those special times we spend together,
Can't be explained in a thousand words,
But the feelings inside,
An expression of one's self,
> So real
>> So true
I could only ask for those special moments,
To share with you can never replace,
Any desire one could ever have,
You are a flower of love,
And to me you are life.